D0847970

BASKETBALL'S GREATEST STARS

RUSSELL WESTBROOK

by Brian Hall

SportsZone

An Imprint of Abdo Publishing
abdopublishing.com

abdopublishing.com

Published by Abdo Publishing, a division of ABDO, PO Box 398166, Minneapolis, Minnesota 55439. Copyright © 2017 by Abdo Consulting Group, Inc. International copyrights reserved in all countries. No part of this book may be reproduced in any form without written permission from the publisher. SportsZone™ is a trademark and logo of Abdo Publishing.

Printed in the United States of America, North Mankato, Minnesota
082016
012017

**THIS BOOK CONTAINS
RECYCLED MATERIALS**

Cover Photos: Marcio Jose Sanchez/AP Images, foreground; Eric Gay/AP Images background
Interior Photos: Marcio Jose Sanchez/AP Images, 1 (foreground), 28, 29; Eric Gay/AP Images 1 (background); Kathy Willens/AP Images, 4-5, 6, 7; Mark Blinch/The Canadian Press/AP Images, 8-9, 26-27; Eric Risberg/AP Images, 10-11; Mark J. Terrill/AP Images, 12-13, 19; Paul Connors/AP Images, 14; Julie Jacobson/AP Images, 15; Sue Ogrocki/AP Images, 16-17; Chris Carlson/AP Images, 18; John Raoux/AP Images, 20-21; Daniel Ochoa de Olza/AP Images, 22; Jeff Roberson/AP Images, 23; Sue Ogrocki/AP Images, 24-25

Editor: Todd Kortemeier
Series Designer: Laura Polzin

Publisher's Cataloging-in-Publication Data
Names: Hall, Brian, author.
Title: Russell Westbrook / by Brian Hall.
Description: Minneapolis, MN : Abdo Publishing, 2017. | Series: Basketball's
    greatest stars | Includes index.
Identifiers: LCCN 2016945486 | ISBN 9781680785487 (lib. bdg.) |
    ISBN 9781680798111 (ebook)
Subjects: LCSH: Westbrook, Russell, 1988- --Juvenile literature. | Basketball
    players--United States--Biography--Juvenile literature.
Classification: DDC 796.323 [B]--dc23
LC record available at http://lccn.loc.gov/2016945486

CONTENTS

SHINING STAR

With his speedy drives to the basket, Russell Westbrook was making defenders look silly. It was the 2015 National Basketball Association (NBA) All-Star Game. And Westbrook looked like the biggest star of all.

The All-Star Game doesn't feature much defense. Westbrook took full advantage. He put his offensive talents on display with a historic All-Star Game effort.

FAST FACT

Westbrook made the All-Star Game five times in his first eight seasons. He averaged 23.8 points per game.

Russell Westbrook drives to the hoop in the 2015 NBA All-Star Game.

Despite not starting the game, Westbrook quickly made an impact. He was everywhere on the court. He hit five three-pointers and scored on two alley-oops. In just 11 minutes, he racked up 27 points. That was a record for points in an All-Star Game half.

In the third quarter, he stole the ball and ran it back for a dunk. He finished with 41 points and was named Most Valuable Player (MVP). Westbrook ended up one point short of the game record set by Wilt Chamberlain in 1962.

Westbrook proudly displays his All-Star Game MVP trophy.

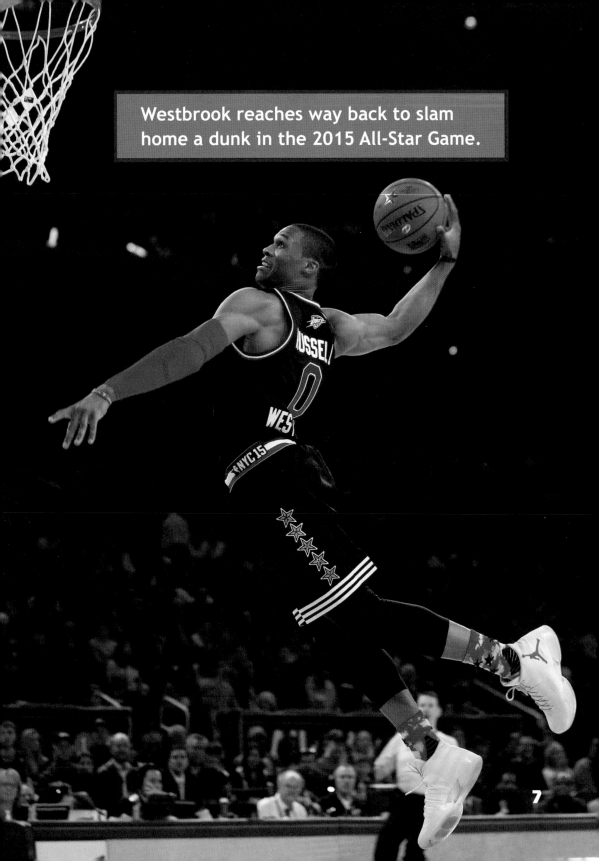

Westbrook reaches way back to slam home a dunk in the 2015 All-Star Game.

Westbrook wasn't done. In 2016 he started the All-Star Game and scored 31 points. He won MVP for a second straight season. He became the first player to win MVP in consecutive years without sharing the award.

Westbrook's breakthrough performance showed he was one of the NBA's elite players.

Westbrook hangs on the rim following a dunk at the 2016 All-Star Game.

FAST FACT

Only five players have won more All-Star MVP awards than Westbrook: Kobe Bryant, Bob Pettit, Michael Jordan, Shaquille O'Neal, and Oscar Robertson.

TRAGEDY AND TRIUMPH

Russell Westbrook was born in Long Beach, California, on November 12, 1988. His NBA potential wasn't easy to see early on. He was just 5-foot-8 (1.7 m) and 140 pounds (63.5 kg) as a freshman at Leuzinger High School in Lawndale, California.

Instead it was a teammate and close friend of Russell's who caught the attention of University of California-Los Angeles (UCLA) coach Ben Howland.

Westbrook, *0*, grew up pretty close to UCLA, but they didn't recruit him until later in high school.

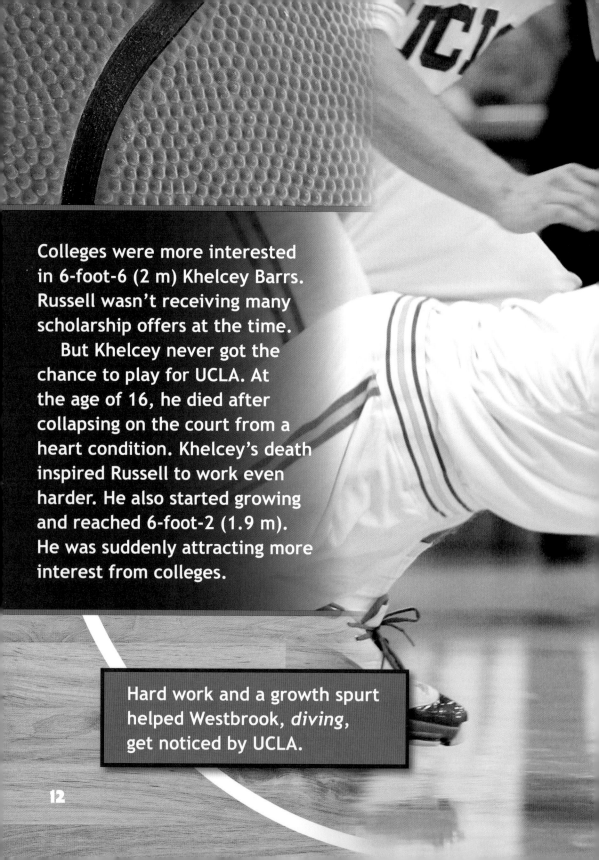

Colleges were more interested in 6-foot-6 (2 m) Khelcey Barrs. Russell wasn't receiving many scholarship offers at the time.

But Khelcey never got the chance to play for UCLA. At the age of 16, he died after collapsing on the court from a heart condition. Khelcey's death inspired Russell to work even harder. He also started growing and reached 6-foot-2 (1.9 m). He was suddenly attracting more interest from colleges.

Hard work and a growth spurt helped Westbrook, *diving*, get noticed by UCLA.

Westbrook eventually chose UCLA. He felt like he was playing for his friend. As a freshman Westbrook was a backup to future NBA draft pick Darren Collison. He started 34 games as a sophomore and averaged 12.7 points per game. UCLA made it to the Final Four in both seasons.

Westbrook showed enough potential to draw interest from NBA teams. He was drafted fourth overall by the Seattle SuperSonics in 2008.

Westbrook was named Defensive Player of the Year for the Pacific-10 Conference in 2008.

Westbrook greets NBA Commissioner David Stern after being drafted by the Sonics.

FAST FACT

Westbrook is active off the court as well. He received the NBA Cares Community Assist award in 2015 for his charity work.

ARRIVAL IN THE NBA

The SuperSonics moved to Oklahoma City before Westbrook played a game for them. Along with second-year player Kevin Durant, Westbrook was one of the stars of the Thunder in their new city. His quickness and jumping ability helped him adjust to the NBA quickly.

Westbrook was named the league's Rookie of the Month in December 2008 and February 2009. He recorded his first triple-double with 17 points, 10 rebounds, and 10 assists in a game that March.

Westbrook never wore a Seattle uniform, instead donning the blue and orange of the Thunder for his first NBA season.

FAST FACT

Westbrook is left-handed except when it comes to shooting a basketball.

It was a sign of things to come for the versatile Westbrook. He averaged 15.3 points, 5.3 assists, 1.3 steals, and 4.9 rebounds per game as a rookie.

Westbrook became one of the NBA's best athletes. His speed and competitiveness gave other teams a lot to worry about. In 2010 Westbrook and the Thunder made their first playoff appearance. The Los Angeles Lakers used star Kobe Bryant to guard Westbrook. The Thunder couldn't pull off the upset and lost in six games.

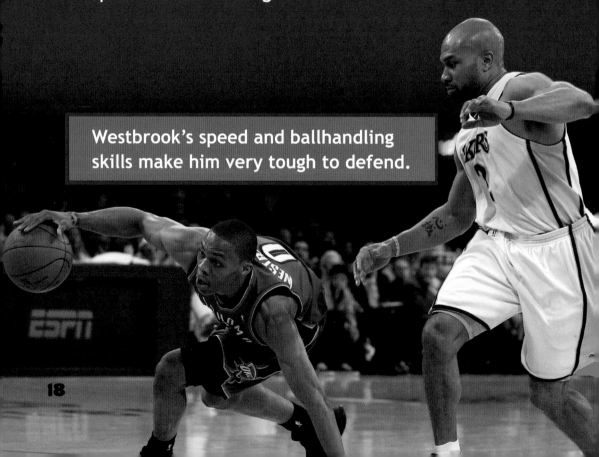

Westbrook's speed and ballhandling skills make him very tough to defend.

Westbrook leaps between two Lakers in his first career playoff game in 2010.

FAST FACT

Westbrook loves clothes and fashion. He has attended Fashion Week in New York and Paris.

MODERN-DAY "MAGIC"

Westbrook admired Lakers great Earvin "Magic" Johnson while growing up in Southern California. Johnson was known as a player who could do it all. He could run the offense, shoot the ball, and pass it.

Westbrook has a similar playing style. Like Johnson, his team's offense runs through him.

FAST FACT

Westbrook finished fourth in MVP voting in 2014-15 and 2015-16.

Opponents have to look out for Westbrook's ability to both pass and score.

In the summer of 2010, Westbrook won a gold medal with Team USA at the Basketball World Cup. But he was still chasing a title with the Thunder. He made his first All-Star Game in 2011. The Thunder made the conference finals before losing to the Dallas Mavericks.

The next year, the dynamic duo of Westbrook and Durant led the Thunder to the NBA Finals. Down two games to one to the Miami Heat, Westbrook dominated with 43 points. But it wasn't enough. The Thunder lost that game and Game 5 to lose the series.

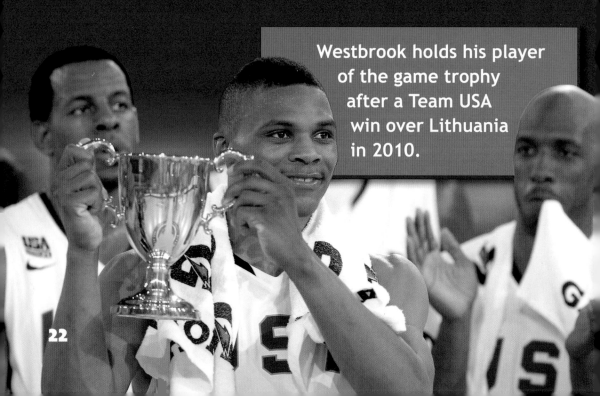

Westbrook holds his player of the game trophy after a Team USA win over Lithuania in 2010.

Thunder fans celebrate with Westbrook in the second half of the first NBA Finals game in Oklahoma City.

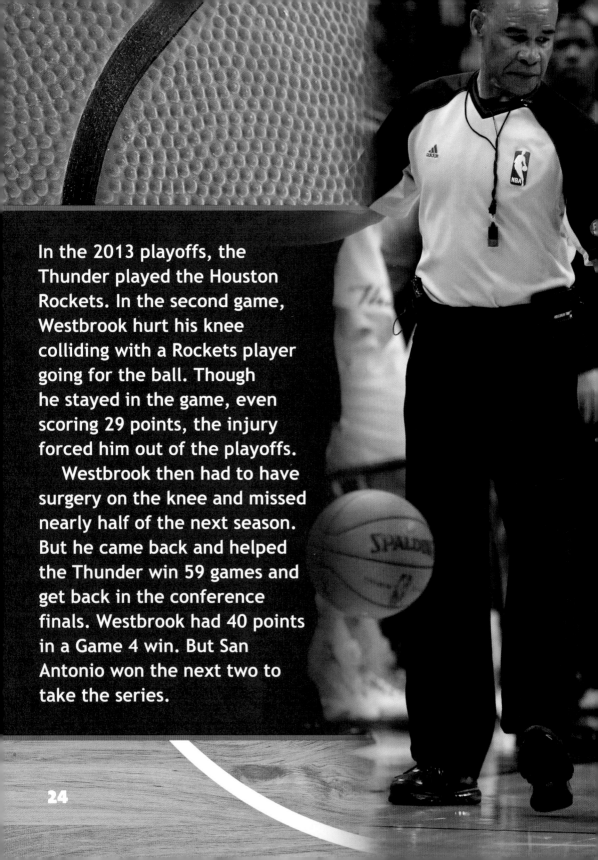

In the 2013 playoffs, the Thunder played the Houston Rockets. In the second game, Westbrook hurt his knee colliding with a Rockets player going for the ball. Though he stayed in the game, even scoring 29 points, the injury forced him out of the playoffs.

Westbrook then had to have surgery on the knee and missed nearly half of the next season. But he came back and helped the Thunder win 59 games and get back in the conference finals. Westbrook had 40 points in a Game 4 win. But San Antonio won the next two to take the series.

The Thunder lost Westbrook in the first round of the 2013 playoffs, and were eliminated in the next round.

CHASING A TITLE

Westbrook's multiple skills meant he was always a threat for a triple-double. He had 11 during the 2014-15 season. In February 2015, he averaged 31.2 points, 9.1 rebounds, and 10.3 assists per game. He became just the second player to average at least 30 points, 8 rebounds, and 10 assists in one month.

Westbrook was even better in 2015-16. He had 18 triple-doubles. That tied Magic Johnson for the most in the previous 50 seasons.

Westbrook celebrates his second consecutive All-Star Game MVP award in 2016.

FAST FACT

Westbrook led the NBA in scoring in 2014-15 with 28.1 points per game. He was also second in steals (2.1) and fourth in assists (8.6) per game.

After missing the playoffs in 2014-15, Westbrook led the Thunder to the conference finals in 2015-16. In Game 4, he had his fifth career playoff triple-double with 36 points, 11 rebounds, and 11 assists. Off a steal, Westbrook hit a 15-footer late that caused Thunder fans to roar. The huge win put the Thunder within one game of the NBA Finals.

But the Golden State Warriors stunned them by winning three in a row to take the series. Westbrook's longtime teammate Kevin Durant left to join the Warriors the next season. Westbrook had to lead the Thunder by himself to try and win a title for Oklahoma City.

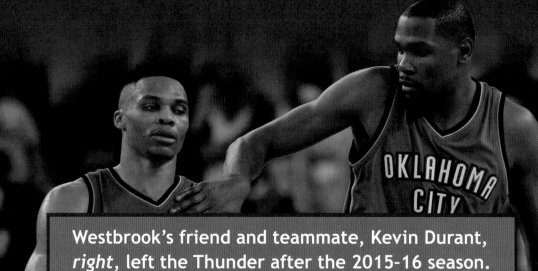

Westbrook's friend and teammate, Kevin Durant, *right*, left the Thunder after the 2015-16 season.

Westbrook goes up for a shot in the 2016 Western Conference Finals.

TIMELINE

1988
Russell Westbrook Jr. is born on November 12 in Long Beach, California.

2004
Westbrook's best friend and teammate Khelcey Barrs collapses on the court and dies.

2006
Westbrook accepts a scholarship and begins playing at UCLA.

2008
Westbrook is drafted fourth overall by the Seattle SuperSonics.

2009
Westbrook finishes fourth in Rookie of the Year voting and is named to the All-Rookie team.

2012
Oklahoma City and Westbrook advance to the NBA Finals for the first time.

2013
The playoffs end early for Westbrook after he suffers a knee injury.

2015
Westbrook is named All-Star Game MVP and leads the NBA in scoring.

2016
Westbrook becomes the first player to win the All-Star Game MVP in back-to-back seasons without sharing the award.

GLOSSARY

ASSIST
A pass that leads directly to a scored basket.

FRESHMAN
A first-year student.

REBOUND
Grabbing a missed shot in basketball.

ROOKIE
A first-year player.

SCHOLARSHIP
Money given to a student to pay for education expenses.

SOPHOMORE
A second-year student.

TRIPLE-DOUBLE
Accumulating 10 or more of three certain statistics in a single game.

UPSET
When a supposedly weaker team beats a stronger team.

INDEX

ABOUT THE AUTHOR

Brian Hall has been a sports reporter for more than a decade. A graduate of the University of Minnesota, he currently lives in Minnesota with his wife and two children.